Sandlot Peanuts

Other Peanuts Books in This Format
Peanuts Treasury
Peanuts Classics
The Snoopy Festival

Sandlot Peanuts

CHARLES M. SCHULZ

With an Introduction by Joe Garagiola

Holt, Rinehart and Winston / New York

Copyright © 1977 by United Feature Syndicate, Inc.

"Peanuts" comic strips: Copr. 1961, 1962, 1963, 1964 © 1965, 1966
1967, 1968, 1969, 1970, 1971, 1972, 1973, 1974, 1975, 1976
by United Feature Syndicate, Inc.

Introduction copyright © 1977 by Joe Garagiola

Published simultaneously in Canada by Holt,
Rinehart and Winston of Canada, Limited.

Library of Congress Catalog Card Number: 77-71363

ISBN: 0-03-022621-X

Printed in the United States of America

1 3 5 7 9 10 8 6 4 2

Introduction
by Joe Garagiola

I enjoy reading most comic strips and I may even become a fan of the characters. But for me, the members of the Peanuts gang are *real* people. I *know* the Peanuts gang. Every strip I read is like a letter from an old friend. And you know an old friend will not only tell you the news, but also give you a zinger every once in a while. Let me show you what I mean.

Peppermint Patty and Charlie Brown once traded ballplayers. Patty traded Marcie in exchange for Snoopy. When Marcie heard about it, she said to Patty, ''I never thought I'd be traded for a beagle.'' Patty's answer was, ''You should be flattered, Marcie. I could have traded you for Joe Garagiola.''

You have this book in your hand—whether you're a buyer, a borrower, or a browser—and that tells me we have something in common. We both look upon the Peanuts gang as friends: Linus, Schroeder, Lucy, Snoopy (they say everybody in America has two dogs—his own and Snoopy), Charlie Brown, and the rest.

In this book, each member of the Peanuts gang looks at the game of baseball from his or her own viewpoint. These range from

Charlie Brown's complete devotion to the game, to the somewhat different philosophy of Marcie, who, at one point, holds up a sign reading: PLAY ME, TRADE ME, KEEP ME, WHO CARES?

They look at baseball, and at life, the way I would like to. Charlie Brown has the perfect philosophy. Even though Lucy calls him—among many other things—"a foul ball in the line drive of life," he listens patiently, then counters with, "Just wait 'til next year." It certainly isn't a winning-is-the-only-thing philosophy—the fact is, his won and lost record couldn't be worse—but he doesn't give up hope. Charlie Brown *has* to be the average guy's hero.

One of my personal favorites is never seen in the strip. He is Charlie Brown's number-one baseball idol, Joe Shlabotnik. Joe's talents as a player are obviously not very good, but, at one point, he does get a job managing a team called the "Waffletown Syrups." Charlie Brown goes to see them play, but he arrives too late. His hero has been fired for calling a squeeze play with nobody on base.

I have made no secret over the years of the fact that I played on bad ball clubs, but Charlie Brown pitches for a team that would make any of my old clubs look like Cincinnati's "Big Red Machine." This isn't hard to understand when you realize that Charlie Brown's team has a catcher who daydreams about Beethoven, a second baseman who drags around a security blanket, and a shortstop who is a beagle—true, a beagle who challenges Babe Ruth's home-run record, who in fact takes over for a while as manager of the team, but, nevertheless, a beagle.

The Peanuts gang is the brainchild of Charlie Schulz, known to his friends as "Sparky." When you think of the fame that Charlie Schulz has achieved, and of all the compliments that have deservedly come his way, you could understand it if he were a little temperamental. Yet he is one of the nicest men I know. Sparky Schulz is a lot like Charlie Brown—win or lose, be nice to everybody who comes your way.

When I read the newspapers there are two things I *never* miss. One is the sports page, and the other is Peanuts. Now I have a whole book of baseball *and* the Peanuts gang. For Linus, happiness is a blanket. For Joe Garagiola, happiness is baseball and Charlie Brown—in other words, this book.

Joe Garagiola

SO IT'S RAINING A LITTLE! YOU CAN'T PLAY RIGHT FIELD WITH AN UMBRELLA OVER YOUR HEAD!

CHONK!

I CAN'T EVEN CRITICIZE GOOD..

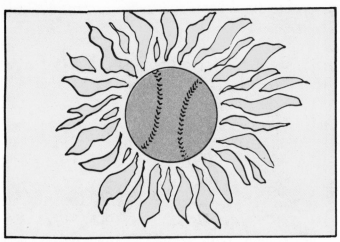

OKAY, TEAM, LET'S GET THIS NEXT GUY!

WE CAN DO IT! WE CAN GET HIM EASY! HE'S NO HITTER! HE'S NO HITTER AT ALL!

C'MON, TEAM, LET'S BEAR DOWN OUT THERE! LET'S REALLY GET THIS GUY!

THAT'S THE ONLY PITCHER I'VE EVER KNOWN WHO SUPPLIED HER OWN INFIELD CHATTER!

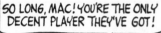

THIS IS RIDICULOUS!

I'VE HIT FIVE HOME RUNS AND PITCHED A NO-HIT GAME, AND WE'RE BEHIND THIRTY-SEVEN TO FIVE! WHOEVER HEARD OF THIRTY-SEVEN UNEARNED RUNS? THIS IS RIDICULOUS!

I THOUGHT I COULD HELP YOUR TEAM, CHUCK, BUT IT'S HOPELESS! I'M GOING BACK WHERE I CAME FROM!

THAT MUST BE A NICE THING TO BE ABLE TO DO...

YOU'RE LEAVING?

OF COURSE, I'M LEAVING! I CAN'T HELP THIS STUPID TEAM!

SO LONG, MAC! YOU'RE THE ONLY DECENT PLAYER THEY'VE GOT!

HE'S A GOOD PLAYER, BUT I STILL THINK HE'S THE FUNNIEST LOOKING KID I'VE EVER SEEN!

DEAR PEPPERMINT PATTY, I HOPE YOU HAD A NICE WALK HOME.

I JUST WANTED YOU TO KNOW THAT I APPRECIATED YOUR COMING CLEAR ACROSS TOWN TO HELP OUR TEAM. SINCERELY,

"CHUCK"

THIS IS A VERY IMPORTANT GAME..

IT'S TRADITIONAL THAT WHOEVER IS IN FIRST PLACE ON THE FOURTH OF JULY GOES ON TO WIN THE PENNANT

POW!

AND WHOEVER IS IN LAST PLACE USUALLY STAYS THERE!

THROW THIS GUY YOUR FAST BALL, CHARLIE BROWN..

I THINK YOU'D BETTER KEEP THE BALL LOW TO THIS GUY, CHARLIE BROWN...GIVE HIM A LOW CURVE..

THROW THIS GUY ALL KNUCKLE BALLS, CHARLIE BROWN...YOU'LL FOOL HIM WITH KNUCKLE BALLS...

THIS IS THE LATEST THING... PITCHING BY COMMITTEE!

IT'S JUST A LITTLE BRUISE... I THINK IT'LL BE ALL RIGHT...

DO I THINK IT'S GOING TO RAIN? NO, I DOUBT IT...THOSE DON'T LOOK LIKE RAIN CLOUDS TO ME..

SUPPERTIME? OH, YES...I THINK WE'LL BE FINISHED WELL BEFORE SUPPERTIME..

SOMETIMES I GET TO PITCH IN-BETWEEN QUESTIONS!

HEY, MANAGER, WAIT! I HAVE A QUESTION..

I'VE BEEN READING ABOUT THIS BASEBALL STADIUM THAT HAS PLASTIC GRASS...HOW COME **WE** DON'T HAVE PLASTIC GRASS?

STANDING OUT HERE IN THE OUTFIELD LIKE THIS, LOTS OF QUESTIONS COME TO YOUR MIND

WELL, WE LOST AGAIN, BUT WHO CARES?

SURE, IT'S ONLY A GAME...WE LOST, BUT SO WHAT? WHO CARES?

JUST WHAT I'VE ALWAYS BEEN AFRAID OF... MY TEAM HAS BUILT UP AN IMMUNITY TO LOSING!

I'M GOING TO TRY FOR A HOME RUN CHARLIE BROWN!

EITHER WE WIN OR WE LOSE! ALL OR NOTHING!

THAT'S THE SPIRIT! GO FOR BROKE!

SYDNEY OR THE BUSH!

"SYDNEY OR THE BUSH"?

HEY, LOOK! YOUR BROTHER IS FLOATING OUT TO SEA ON THE PITCHER'S MOUND!

YOU SHOULD WAVE TO HIM...YOU'LL PROBABLY NEVER SEE HIM AGAIN...

SO LONG, BROTHER'!
WHO'S GOING TO FEED THE DOG?

FLOATING OUT TO SEA ON A PITCHER'S MOUND... I CAN'T BELIEVE IT!

CHARLIE BROWN'S IN TROUBLE, SNOOPY... WE SHOULD DO SOMETHING...
THAT'S TRUE!

IF HE'S NOT GOING TO BE AROUND TO FEED ME ANY MORE, MAYBE I SHOULD PLANT A GARDEN...

LET'S SEE, I COULD PUT SOME TOMATOES HERE, AND SOME CORN OVER THERE AND MAYBE SOME RADISHES HERE...

HELP! I'M FLOATING OUT TO SEA!
HELP! SOMEBODY SAVE ME!

HANG ON, CHARLIE BROWN! I HAVE GOOD NEWS FOR YOU! YOU'RE NOT FLOATING OUT TO SEA....

YOU'RE FLOATING DOWN A DRIVEWAY AND INTO AN ALLEY BEHIND A SUPERMARKET!

LAND HO!

WHAT ARE YOU DOING HOME?

I THOUGHT YOU HAD FLOATED OUT TO SEA...

NO, I GUESS NOT...I ENDED UP IN AN ALLEY BEHIND A SUPERMARKET...IT WAS A TERRIBLE EXPERIENCE...

I SUPPOSE YOU'RE GOING TO WANT YOUR ROOM BACK..

THIS NEXT GUY IS STRONG, CHARLIE BROWN

DON'T THROW HIM ANYTHING HE CAN HIT...

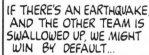

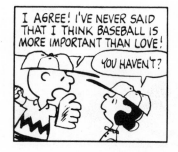

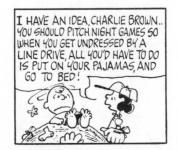

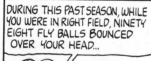

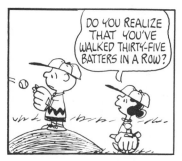

MY DAD IS PLAYING IN A CANCER FUND GOLF TOURNAMENT TOMORROW...

MY MOM IS PLAYING IN A TENNIS TOURNAMENT NEXT WEEK FOR THE KIDNEY FOUNDATION...

WE SHOULD HOLD A BENEFIT BASEBALL TOURNAMENT

THAT'S A GREAT IDEA!

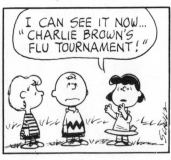
I CAN SEE IT NOW... "CHARLIE BROWN'S FLU TOURNAMENT!"

HELLO, PEPPERMINT PATTY?

HI, CHUCK! GEE, WHAT A SURPRISE... HOW'VE Y'BEEN?

FINE, THANK YOU... I'LL GET RIGHT TO THE POINT... HOW ABOUT YOUR TEAM PLAYING OUR TEAM IN A BENEFIT BASEBALL GAME, YOU KNOW, LIKE THEY HAVE FOR HEART ASSOCIATIONS AND THINGS?

WHAT WOULD OUR GAME BE FOR, CHUCK, THE COMMON COLD?

IF WE'RE GOING TO HAVE A CHARITY BASEBALL GAME, CHARLIE BROWN, IT SHOULD BE FOR A WORTHY CAUSE..

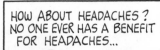
HOW ABOUT HEADACHES? NO ONE EVER HAS A BENEFIT FOR HEADACHES...

HOW ABOUT SORE THROATS? OR HOW ABOUT CUT FINGERS AND SKINNED KNEES?

IF OUR TEAM IS GOING TO BE PLAYING, IT SHOULD BE FOR STOMACH-ACHES!

I CAN'T STAND IT!

GUESS WHAT, MARCIE...OUR TEAM IS GOING TO PLAY CHUCK'S TEAM IN A CHARITY BASEBALL GAME!

BUT I'M NOT ON YOUR TEAM, SIR.. I DON'T PLAY BASEBALL...

WE DON'T WANT YOU TO PLAY MARCIE..WE WANT YOU TO SELL TICKETS!

YOU MEAN GO FROM DOOR TO DOOR?

SURE

WHAT IF I GET MUGGED?

OKAY, MARCIE, HERE ARE THE TICKETS...GET OUT THERE, AND SELL THEM!

THESE TICKETS COST FIFTY CENTS, SIR...WHO'S GOING TO PAY FIFTY CENTS TO WATCH CHUCK'S TEAM PLAY BALL?

YOURS IS NOT TO REASON WHY, MARCIE! YOURS IS TO SELL TICKETS! THIS IS FOR CHARITY!

I'M SORRY, SIR... I GUESS I'M ALWAYS "REASONING WHY"

STOP CALLING ME "SIR"!

GOOD MORNING, MA'AM... I'M SELLING TICKETS TO A CHARITY BASEBALL GAME, AND I...

THE CHARITY? STOMACH-ACHES!

SLAM!

THIS COULD TURN OUT TO BE KIND OF DIFFICULT

GOOD AFTERNOON, MA'AM... I'M SELLING TICKETS TO A CHARITY BASEBALL GAME...

THE CHARITY? STOMACH-ACHES!

SLAM!!

STOMACH-ACHES ARE A LEGITIMATE CHARITY!!

JUST THINK, CHUCK, OUR CHARITY BASEBALL GAME IS NEXT WEEK!

I'M VERY EXCITED... I THINK IT'S GOING TO BE THE BIGGEST THING EVER!

YOU AND YOUR STUPID BALL GAME! HAVE YOU EVER TRIED TO SELL TICKETS TO A STOMACH-ACHE?!!

NOBODY WANTS TO COME TO YOUR STUPID OL' BALL GAME! I'M TIRED OF HAVING DOORS SLAMMED IN MY FACE!!

I COULD HAVE BEEN MUGGED! A STOMACH-ACHE IS NO KIND OF CHARITY! I HATE SELLING TICKETS! I HATE BASEBALL!

I TRIED TO SELL THOSE TICKETS!

I REALLY TRIED, BUT EVERY PLACE I WENT THEY SLAMMED THE DOOR IN MY FACE!! I COULDN'T TAKE IT!!!

I TRIED AND TRIED AND TRIED! WAAH!!!

SMAK

POOR, SWEET BABY!

I'M A FAILURE, SNOOPY... I DIDN'T SELL A SINGLE TICKET!

POOR, SWEET BABY!

SMAK!

WELL, THERE GOES OUR CHARITY BASEBALL GAME! IF NO ONE BUYS A TICKET, WE MIGHT AS WELL CALL IT OFF...

POOR, SWEET BABY!

SMAK!

RATS! I NEVER DO ANYTHING RIGHT... NOTHING EVER WORKS OUT FOR ME...

Charlie Brown: YESTERDAY MORNING I WOKE UP VERY EARLY... I JUST COULDN'T SLEEP...

Sign: PSYCHIATRIC HELP 5¢ — THE DOCTOR IS IN

Charlie Brown: MY BEDROOM FACES EAST, AND SO I COULD SEE THE SUN COMING UP... ONLY, IT WASN'T THE SUN... IT WAS A HUGE **BASEBALL**!

Charlie Brown: I THINK I MUST BE CRACKING UP... I THINK I'M FINALLY LOSING MY MIND... AND ON TOP OF IT ALL, I FEEL TERRIBLY ALONE...

Sign: THE DOCTOR IS IN

Lucy: OKAY, NOW TELL ME MORE ABOUT THIS HUGE BASEBALL..

Sally: THERE'S A FULL MOON TONIGHT, BIG BROTHER..

Sally: YOU SHOULD GO OUT, AND LOOK AT IT
Charlie Brown: MAYBE I WILL...THANK YOU..

Sally: HOW ABOUT AN ICE CREAM CONE, BIG BROTHER?

Charlie Brown: THAT WOULD BE VERY NICE, THANK YOU..

Sally: ONE ICE CREAM CONE COMING UP!

Charlie Brown: EVERYTHING I SEE LOOKS LIKE A BASEBALL TO ME...

Charlie Brown: AND NOW MY HEAD HAS STARTED TO ITCH... I THINK I HAVE A RASH OR SOMETHING...

Linus: TURN AROUND... LET ME LOOK..

Linus: I THINK YOU'D BETTER SEE YOUR PEDIATRICIAN, CHARLIE BROWN!

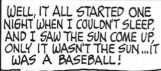

YES, MA'AM, I HAVE AN APPOINTMENT TO SEE THE DOCTOR...

WELL, IT ALL STARTED ONE NIGHT WHEN I COULDN'T SLEEP, AND I SAW THE SUN COME UP, ONLY IT WASN'T THE SUN...IT WAS A BASEBALL!

WHY DO I HAVE THIS SACK OVER MY HEAD? WELL, I'VE ALSO DEVELOPED THIS RASH OR SOMETHING, YOU SEE, AND...

MA'AM, DO WE HAVE TO DISCUSS THIS IN FRONT OF THE WHOLE OFFICE?

I APPRECIATE YOUR SEEING ME, DOCTOR, BECAUSE I THINK I NEED A LOT OF HELP...

I HAVE THIS RASH OR SOMETHING, AND IT MAKES MY HEAD LOOK LIKE A BASEBALL...

WHY AM I WEARING THIS SACK?

SOMEONE TRIED TO AUTOGRAPH MY HEAD!

WELL, DOCTOR, IT ALL STARTED EARLY ONE MORNING WHEN I SAW THE SUN COME UP...

"ONLY IT WASN'T THE SUN... IT WAS A HUGE BASEBALL!"

THEN IT WAS THE MOON, AND PRETTY SOON EVERYTHING LOOKED LIKE A BASEBALL TO ME, AND THEN I GOT THIS RASH OR SOMETHING ON MY HEAD, AND...WELL...

AM I CRACKING UP, DOCTOR? IS THIS THE LAST OF THE NINTH?

WHAT ARE YOU PACKING FOR, BIG BROTHER?

MY DOCTOR SAYS I SHOULD GO TO CAMP...HE SAID I HAVE TO DO SOMETHING THAT WILL TAKE MY MIND OFF BASEBALL

I'VE SEEN YOU PLAY.. I NEVER THOUGHT YOU HAD YOUR MIND ON IT!

THANKS A LOT... I'LL SEE YOU IN TWO WEEKS...

YOU'RE GOING TO BE A BIG HIT AT CAMP CARRYING YOUR HEAD IN A SACK!!

DON'T JUST STAND THERE, KID...THERE'S A MEETING OVER AT THE MAIN BUILDING!

EVERYTHING ALWAYS HAPPENS SO FAST AT CAMP..I NEVER KNOW WHAT'S GOING ON...

WHAT'S THIS MEETING ALL ABOUT?

WE HAVE TO ELECT A CAMP PRESIDENT

I'VE GOT A GREAT IDEA... LET'S NOMINATE THE KID HERE WITH THE SACK OVER HIS HEAD!

HMM..

SOMETHING IS MISSING, YOU KNOW THAT, CHUCK?

THIS IS OUR FIRST GAME OF THE SEASON, AND WE DON'T HAVE ANY OPENING-DAY CEREMONIES...

I REMEMBER ONCE I SAW A GAME ON TV WHERE THEY RELEASED A HUGE FLOCK OF PIGEONS THAT SOARED UP INTO THE SKY, AND THEN FLEW IN GREAT CIRCLES AROUND THE STADIUM...WE NEED SOMETHING LIKE THAT

WE HAVE A SURPRISE FOR YOU... OPEN THE CAGE, SNOOPY..

THAT'S NOT THE SAME THING AT ALL, CHUCK!

WE'RE THE HOME TEAM, CHUCK, SO YOU GUYS BAT FIRST, AND WE'LL TAKE THE FIELD..

OKAY, SNOOPY, YOU'RE OUR LEAD-OFF BATTER...LET'S START THINGS OFF BIG...

BUT LOOK OUT FOR PEPPERMINT PATTY...SHE'S A GOOD PITCHER!

HERE WE GO! THE FIRST PITCH OF THE SEASON! I LOVE BASEBALL!

BONK!!

WHAT KIND OF A GAME ARE YOU PLAYING?! YOU BEANED MY BEST PLAYER!

I DIDN'T DO IT ON PURPOSE, CHUCK...HE WAS CROWDING THE PLATE...I WAS JUST TRYING TO BRUSH HIM BACK!

FORGET IT! I'M TAKING MY TEAM HOME!

YOU CAN'T FORFEIT THE GAME, CHUCK!

IF YOU GO HOME, YOU LOSE! DON'T FORFEIT THE GAME, CHUCK!

I'M DISGRACED! WINNING A GAME FROM CHUCK'S TEAM BY FORFEIT IS THE MOST DEGRADING THING THAT CAN HAPPEN TO A MANAGER!

MAYBE YOU COULD FORFEIT THE FORFEIT, SIR..

STOP CALLING ME "SIR"!

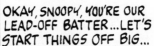

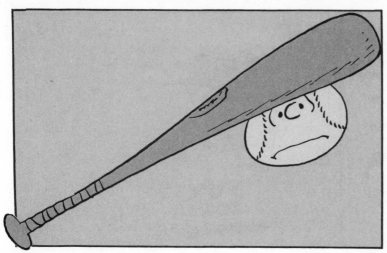

ANOTHER GAME TODAY...IF WE WIN, WE'LL ONLY BE TEN GAMES OUT OF SEVENTH PLACE...

WHY DO YOU ALWAYS PUT YOUR LEFT SHOE ON FIRST, BIG BROTHER?

WELL, ACTUALLY, I DON'T...I ONLY PUT IT ON FIRST ON DAYS WHEN WE HAVE A BASEBALL GAME...

I GUESS IT'S KIND OF A SUPERSTITION... BASEBALL PLAYERS HAVE A LOT OF SUPERSTITIONS..

WHAT WOULD HAPPEN IF YOU DIDN'T DO IT?

WELL, WE'D PROBABLY LOSE THE GAME

HAVE YOU EVER WON?

WHERE'S OUR PITCHER?

I DON'T KNOW...I HAVEN'T SEEN HIM..

!?

I DON'T UNDERSTAND...THE GAME IS READY TO START, AND YOU'RE STILL SITTING HERE IN YOUR BEDROOM WITHOUT YOUR SHOES ON!

THIS IS RIDICULOUS

STUPID IS THE WORD!

IT'S NEVER GOING TO STOP RAINING! I'M GOING HOME!

BUT WHAT ABOUT THE GAME?

IT'LL PROBABLY CLEAR UP ANY MINUTE NOW... I THINK I SEE THE SUN..

WHERE'S EVERYONE GOING? DON'T GO! WE HAVE A GAME TO PLAY! COME BACK!!

YOU'RE OUT OF YOUR MIND, CHARLIE BROWN! ANYONE WHO WOULD STAND OUT IN THIS RAIN SHOULD SEE A PSYCHIATRIST!

MAYBE SHE'S RIGHT...

WELL, HELLO, THERE...WHAT CAN I DO FOR YOU?

PSYCHIATRIC HELP 5¢

THE DOCTOR IS IN

I THINK THERE MUST BE SOMETHING WRONG WITH ME...I DON'T SEEM TO KNOW ENOUGH TO GET IN OUT OF THE RAIN..

THAT'S VERY INTERESTING..

I JUST GET SO INVOLVED IN THESE BASEBALL GAMES I JUST SORT OF FORGET EVERYTHING ELSE, AND I JUST KIND OF LOSE TRACK OF EVERYTHING AND..

YOU KNOW WHAT?

WHAT?

THE DOCTOR IS IN

I'M GETTING WET!

THE DOCTOR

IT'S A MISTAKE TO TRY TO AVOID THE UNPLEASANT THINGS IN LIFE..

POW!

BUT I'M BEGINNING TO CONSIDER IT...

YOU KNOW, I JUST THOUGHT OF SOMETHING THAT MAY HELP OUR TEAM..

IF WE COME IN LAST PLACE, THAT MEANS WE'LL GET FIRST CHOICE IN THE PLAYER DRAFT

THE LAST TIME THAT HAPPENED WE GOT STUCK WITH THAT STUPID BEAGLE..

YOU'LL ALWAYS BE FIRST CHOICE IN MY PLAYER DRAFT, SWEETIE!
SMAK♥

CHARLIE BROWN, DO YOU REMEMBER THAT TEAM THAT BEAT US FORTY-ONE TO NOTHING?

DO YOU REMEMBER HOW, AFTER THAT GAME, YOU WENT AROUND SHOUTING, "JUST WAIT 'TIL NEXT YEAR"?

WELL, THIS IS THAT NEXT YEAR

YOU SHOULD TRY NOT TO REMEMBER THOSE THINGS!

POW!

EVERY NOW AND THEN I BECOME PLAGUED BY SELF-DOUBTS...

HEY, MANAGER, HOLD IT A MINUTE!

AS LONG AS I HAVE TO STAND IN THE OUTFIELD, I THOUGHT I MIGHT AS WELL GO BAREFOOTED...KEEP AN EYE ON MY SHOES FOR ME, WILL YOU?

MAYBE YOU WANT ME TO HAVE THEM BRONZED!!

WHAT A SARCASTIC MANAGER!

* SIGH *

HERE'S MY OL' PITCHER'S MOUND... COVERED WITH SNOW...

THIS MOUND AND I HAVE BEEN IN SOME GREAT BALL GAMES

WHAT MEMORIES....

I'LL NEVER FORGET THAT GAME WHEN THE OTHER TEAM CAME TO BAT IN THE LAST HALF OF THE NINTH INNING, AND..

OKAY, EVERYBODY! STAND BACK! THIS IS IT!

HERE SHE GOES THROUGH THE STARTING GATE...THE WIND RUSHING THROUGH HER HAIR! IT'S THE LADIES CHAMPION! IT'S THE DOWNHILL RACER!!!!!!

..AND THEY NEEDED ONLY ONE RUN TO TIE THE GAME.. THERE I WAS...

LUNCH TIME AGAIN..

I REMEMBER HOW I USED TO SIT ON THIS BENCH EVERY NOON AND STARE ACROSS THE PLAYGROUND AT THAT LITTLE RED-HAIRED GIRL...

ALL I WANTED WAS TO BE ABLE TO SIT NEXT TO HER AND TALK TO HER...JUST BE WITH HER..THAT WASN'T ASKING TOO MUCH, WAS IT? BUT IT NEVER HAPPENED...

AND THEN SHE MOVED AWAY, AND NOW I DON'T EVEN KNOW WHERE SHE LIVES, AND SHE DOESN'T EVEN KNOW I EXIST, AND I SIT HERE EVERY DAY, AND I WONDER WHAT SHE'S DOING, AND I ..

HI, CHARLIE BROWN..WHAT ARE YOU DOING, SITTING HERE PLANNING ANOTHER BASEBALL SEASON? THAT'S ALL YOU THINK ABOUT, ISN'T IT?

BASEBALL ISN'T THE WHOLE WORLD, YOU KNOW... THAT'S YOUR TROUBLE..YOU NEVER THINK ABOUT ANYTHING ELSE!

YOU MUST BE INSENSITIVE OR SOMETHING

✕ SIGH ✕

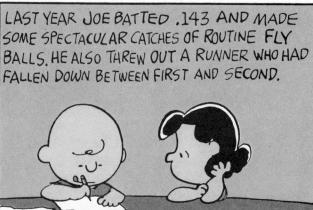

THAT CHUCK..HE'S SOMETHING ELSE...

I DON'T KNOW WHY I EVEN THINK ABOUT HIM..

CHUCK JUST DOESN'T SEEM TO UNDERSTAND A GIRL'S EMOTIONS...

IN FACT, CHUCK DOESN'T SEEM TO UNDERSTAND GIRLS AT ALL..

CHUCK IS HARD TO TALK TO BECAUSE HE DOESN'T UNDERSTAND LIFE..

HE DOESN'T UNDERSTAND LAUGHING AND CRYING

HE DOESN'T UNDERSTAND LOVE, AND SILLY TALK, AND TOUCHING HANDS, AND THINGS LIKE THAT..

HE PLAYS A LOT OF BASEBALL, BUT I DOUBT IF HE EVEN UNDERSTANDS BASEBALL...

KNOCK KNOCK KNOCK

I DON'T THINK YOU UNDERSTAND ANYTHING, CHUCK!

I DON'T EVEN UNDERSTAND WHAT IT IS I DON'T UNDERSTAND

YOU WANTED ME, MANAGER?

I SURE DO..

I THINK YOU NEED A LITTLE PRACTICE ON FLY BALLS, LUCY, SO IF YOU'LL GET OUT THERE, I'LL HIT YOU A FEW...

JUST TROT ON OUT THERE, AND I'LL HIT SOME HIGH ONES, AND WE'LL SEE HOW YOU DO...

WELL, GO ON! GET OUT THERE BEFORE I HIT ONE AND YOU HAVE TO CHASE IT!

I'M WARNING YOU..I'M NOT GONNA WAIT! I'LL JUST GO AHEAD AND WHACK ONE SO FAR YOU'LL HAVE TO RUN FIFTY MILES!

GO AHEAD! GET MOVING! GET OUT THERE BEFORE I SWING BECAUSE I'M NOT WAITING ANOTHER SECOND!

YOU'D BETTER START MOVING.. HERE IT GOES!!

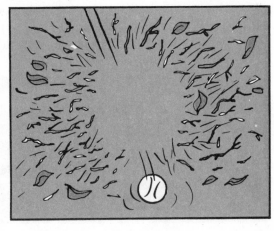

IS THIS SOMETHING UNUSUAL, OR DO ALL PITCHERS FLOAT?

HERE, CHARLIE BROWN... SIGN THIS PETITION!

WHAT'S IT FOR?

DON'T BE SO WISHY-WASHY.. JUST SIGN IT!

WANTING TO KNOW WHAT YOU'RE SIGNING IS NOT BEING WISHY-WASHY!

WHY ARE YOU SO CRABBY?

YELLING AT SOMEONE WHO SAYS YOU'RE WISHY-WASHY FOR WANTING TO KNOW WHAT YOU'RE SIGNING BEFORE YOU SIGN IT, IS NOT BEING CRABBY!!

ALL RIGHT, IF I LET YOU READ IT, WILL YOU SIGN IT?

"WE, THE UNDERSIGNED, THINK OUR MANAGER IS TOO WISHY-WASHY AND TOO CRABBY"

YOU PROMISED TO SIGN IT..

I'M THE ONLY PERSON I KNOW WHO'S EVER SIGNED A PETITION AGAINST HIMSELF

CLOMP!

CLOMP!

CLOMP!

CLOMP!

CLOMP!

CLOMP!

CLOMP!

I THINK I'LL SLEEP IN TOMORROW MORNING... I HAVE TIRED TEETH!

SOMETIMES, WHEN I'M OUT HERE ON THE MOUND PITCHING, A **VERY** PECULIAR THING HAPPENS..

SOMETIMES I START THINKING ABOUT THAT LITTLE RED-HAIRED GIRL..

HERE I AM, SURROUNDED BY KIDS PLAYING BASEBALL ..EVERYONE IS YELLING AND SCREAMING AND RUNNING AROUND, AND WHAT AM I DOING? I'M PITCHING, BUT I'M THINKING ABOUT HER

I'M THINKING ABOUT HOW I'LL PROBABLY NEVER **SEE** HER AGAIN, AND ABOUT HOW UNFAIR IT IS, AND I FEEL LIKE SITTING DOWN AND CRYING...

I STAND OUT HERE, AND I THROW THE BALL, AND I THINK ABOUT HOW HAPPY I COULD BE IF I WERE HER FRIEND, AND IF I COULD BE WITH HER, AND SHE LIKED ME.. AND...

SOMETIMES I ALMOST FORGET WHERE I AM...

GET THE BALL OVER THE PLATE, YOU BLOCKHEAD!

ALMOST

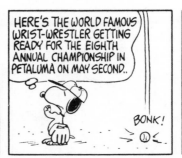

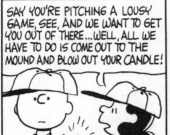

ALL RIGHT, TEAM, THIS IS THE BEGINNING OF A NEW SEASON!

IF WE ALL WORK TOGETHER, THIS CAN BE OUR GREATEST YEAR

NOW, THE FIRST THING WE HAVE TO DO IS START A PROGRAM OF VIGOROUS CALISTHENICS...

HOW ABOUT ONE PUSH-UP?

HI, MANAGER! I'M THE TEAM REPRESENTATIVE..

AS SPOKESMAN FOR THE TEAM, MAY I WISH YOU THE VERY BEST OF LUCK DURING THE NEW SEASON

WELL, THANK YOU....

SPEAKING JUST FOR MYSELF, MAY I SAY YOU'RE GOING TO NEED IT!

ALL RIGHT! EVERYBODY OUT FOR A LITTLE INFIELD PRACTICE!

I'LL HIT THE BALL TO THIRD BASE..YOU THROW IT TO FIRST..FIRST THROWS IT HOME, THE CATCHER WHIPS IT BACK TO THIRD AND WE THROW IT AROUND THE HORN! OKAY? LET'S GET IT RIGHT THE FIRST TIME! OKAY, HERE WE GO!!

CLIP

JUST LOOK AT THAT, WILL YOU?

OUR TEAM ISN'T READY TO START A NEW SEASON... WE'RE JUST NOT READY...

WHERE DID THE TIME GO? WHY DOES THE SEASON HAVE TO START SO SOON?

CHARLIE BROWN, OUR TEAM WOULDN'T BE READY IF THE SEASON STARTED IN NOVEMBER!

HERE WE GO... THE FIRST PITCH OF THE NEW SEASON...

POW!

SOMETIMES I HAVE DIFFICULTY TELLING ONE SEASON FROM ANOTHER...

HELLO?

HELLO, CHUCK? THIS IS OL' PEPPERMINT PATTY! HAVE I GOT A SURPRISE FOR YOU! I'VE FOUND YOU A NEW BALLPLAYER....

THIS GUY IS TERRIFIC! HE'S NOT VERY BIG, BUT HE CAN REALLY PLAY! HIS NAME?

JOSÉ PETERSON!

CHUCK, I'D LIKE TO HAVE YOU MEET JOSÉ PETERSON..

NOW, THE WAY I SEE IT, CHUCK, YOU CAN PLAY JOSÉ PETERSON HERE AT SECOND WHERE HE CAN WORK WITH THAT FUNNY-LOOKING KID YOU'VE GOT PLAYING SHORTSTOP...

WHAT ABOUT LINUS? HE'S ALWAYS PLAYED A PRETTY GOOD SECOND BASE...

DON'T WORRY ABOUT LINUS... I'LL EXPLAIN THE WHOLE THING TO HIM..

HI, SWEETIE!

NOW, LOOK, CHUCK... HERE'S THE WAY YOUR NEW LINEUP CAN GO...

WITH JOSÉ PETERSON AT SECOND AND ME TAKING OVER THE MOUND CHORES, YOU'RE GOING TO HAVE A GREAT TEAM, YES SIR!

NOBODY WILL BE ABLE TO BEAT US! WHY, YOU'LL PROBABLY BE SELECTED "MANAGER OF THE YEAR"!

FOR WHAT?

HOW DO YOU LIKE PLAYING IN THE OUTFIELD, CHARLIE BROWN?

TERRIBLE! I'D RATHER BE UP THERE ON THE MOUND..

WE HAVE A BETTER TEAM NOW, BUT IT ISN'T MY TEAM...I THINK I'LL JUST HAVE TO TELL PEPPERMINT PATTY THAT I PREFER TO RUN THIS TEAM MYSELF

✳AHEM✳ EXCUSE ME...YOU...UH... YOU'RE...UH... YOU'RE PITCHING A GREAT GAME...

THANKS, "CHUCK," OL' PAL...

WHAT HAPPENED?

I WAS SUDDENLY OVERCOME BY A BURST OF WISHY-WASHINESS!

I'VE GOT BAD NEWS "CHUCK"...JOSÉ PETERSON AND I HAVE DECIDED TO FORM A TEAM IN OUR OWN NEIGHBORHOOD...

FRANKLY, I DON'T THINK YOUR TEAM IS EVER GOING TO AMOUNT TO MUCH, "CHUCK"...YOU JUST DON'T HAVE IT... MAYBE YOU COULD TRY SHUFFLEBOARD OR SOMETHING LIKE THAT...

WELL, WE'VE GOT A LONG WAY TO GO SO WE'D BETTER SAY GOOD-BY... JOSÉ PETERSON'S MOM IS HAVING ME OVER TONIGHT FOR TORTILLAS AND SWEDISH MEAT-BALLS!

"SHUFFLEBOARD"?!

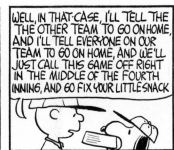

AH! HE HIT IT RIGHT TO MY SHORTSTOP! THIS'LL BE AN EASY OUT...

HERE'S THE WORLD WAR I FLYING ACE ZOOMING THROUGH THE AIR IN HIS SOPWITH CAMEL..

* SIGH *

ONE HUNDRED AND TWENTY-THREE TO NOTHING!

NO ONE SHOULD EVER HAVE TO LOSE THE FIRST GAME OF THE SEASON BY A SCORE OF 123 TO 0!

IT'S JUST NOT RIGHT..

BESIDES, HOW COULD WE POSSIBLY LOSE A GAME 123 TO 0?
WE NEVER GOT ANY BREAKS!

HEY, MANAGER, I HAVE A REQUEST..

TRY TO PITCH SO THAT NO ONE HITS ME A FLY BALL THIS INNING...I DON'T HAVE ANY ROOM IN MY GLOVE FOR A FLY BALL...

WHAT'S THAT YOU HAVE IN IT?

TAPIOCA PUDDING!

THIS MAY BE MY LAST GAME, CHARLIE BROWN

MY DAD'S BEEN TRANSFERRED...WE'RE MOVING TO A NEW CITY...I'LL PROBABLY NEVER SEE YOU AGAIN...

UNLESS, OF COURSE, WE HAPPEN TO GO TO THE SAME COLLEGE..WHAT COLLEGE DO YOU THINK YOU'LL BE GOING TO?

IT'S KIND OF HARD TO DECIDE IN THE LAST HALF OF THE NINTH INNING

PTUI!

I WORRY ABOUT WHO'S GOING TO SEE HIM FIRST...A BIG-LEAGUE SCOUT OR THE HUMANE SOCIETY!

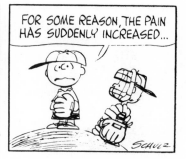

HEY, CHUCK, ARE YOU INTERESTED IN DOING A LITTLE BASEBALL TRADING?

I REALLY NEED A NEW SHORTSTOP THIS YEAR..I'M WILLING TO TRADE MARCIE FOR SNOOPY...HOW ABOUT IT?

WELL, I'M NOT SURE IF YOU...

IT'S A DEAL, HUH, CHUCK? MARCIE FOR SNOOPY!

SIR, YOU DIDN'T TELL HIM THAT I HATE BASEBALL!

SIR, I THINK YOU'RE TAKING ADVANTAGE OF CHUCK...

DON'T BE SILLY, MARCIE!

CHUCK'S TEAM IS SO BAD ALREADY, YOU CAN'T POSSIBLY HURT IT, AND I REALLY NEED SNOOPY ON MY TEAM...

I NEVER THOUGHT I'D BE TRADED FOR A BEAGLE...

YOU SHOULD BE FLATTERED, MARCIE...

I COULD HAVE TRADED YOU FOR JOE GARAGIOLA!

HI, CHUCK, I BROUGHT YOUR NEW PLAYER OVER!

WHERE'S MY SHORTSTOP?

OUT IN BACK... YOU'RE STILL SURE YOU WANT TO TRADE?

DON'T TRY TO GET OUT OF IT, CHUCK! A DEAL IS A DEAL IS A DEAL! JUST SHOW ME MY NEW SHORTSTOP...

CHUCK, YOU HORSE THIEF!

YOU TRADED ME A PLAYER WITH A BROKEN LEG!!

ACTUALLY, IT'S ONLY A FRACTURED METATARSAL

I'VE BEEN ROBBED! I'VE BEEN CHEATED!

I'M GONNA WRITE A LETTER TO THE COMMISSIONER OF BASEBALL!

MAKE SURE YOU SPELL MY NAME RIGHT, SWEETIE!

THIS IS TERRIBLE!

IF THERE'S ANYTHING I DON'T NEED, IT'S A SHORTSTOP WITH HIS LEG IN A CAST!

THIS IS GONNA RUIN ALL THE PLANS I HAD FOR THE BASEBALL SEASON

THINK OF HOW I FEEL... I PROBABLY WON'T BE ABLE TO PLAY AT WIMBLEDON THIS YEAR...

WELL! DID THAT NASTY OL' POP FLY AWAKEN YOU? DID IT DISTURB YOUR BEAUTY SLEEP?

I'M SORRY IF THE SOUND OF FLY BALLS LANDING BEHIND YOU IS DEPRIVING YOU OF YOUR REST!

PERHAPS WE SHOULD SOFTEN THE INFIELD SO THE BALL WON'T MAKE SO MUCH NOISE WHEN IT LANDS BEHIND YOU...

WAAH!

OH, GOOD GRIEF! NOW, I'VE HURT HIS FEELINGS...

I'M SORRY, SNOOPY.. I APOLOGIZE..I SHOULDN'T HAVE BEEN SO SARCASTIC.. I GUESS I DON'T KNOW HOW TO HANDLE PLAYERS...I'M A TERRIBLE MANAGER...I APOLOGIZE..

SNIF

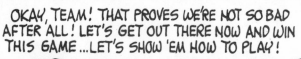

GOOD GRIEF, IT'S ALMOST NOON!

WE HAVE TO SUIT-UP FOR THE BALL GAME, SNOOPY..

HERE'S YOUR CAP...IS MINE ON RIGHT? I WANT IT STRAIGHT, BUT NOT TOO STRAIGHT...

YOURS SHOULD BE TURNED A LITTLE MORE TO THE LEFT..NOT TOO FAR BACK, EITHER, BUT NOT TOO FAR FORWARD...

WHAT DIFFERENCE DOES IT MAKE?

WHAT DIFFERENCE DOES IT MAKE? IT MAKES A LOT OF DIFFERENCE!

GIRLS JUST DON'T UNDERSTAND "SUITING-UP"!

CRACK!

CLOMP!

IN APPRECIATION OF THE GREAT PLAY YOU MADE THIS AFTERNOON, SNOOPY, THE TEAM HAS ASKED ME TO PRESENT YOU THIS...

HOW NICE...THE "GOLDEN MOUTH" AWARD!

IS THIS YOUR BAT, CHARLIE BROWN? IT DOESN'T HAVE YOUR NAME ON IT...

YOU SHOULD HAVE YOUR NAME ON YOURS LIKE ALL OF THE BIG-LEAGUE PLAYERS

LINUS HAS A WOOD-BURNING SET AT HOME... WHY DON'T I TAKE YOUR BAT, AND PUT YOUR NAME ON IT?

SAY! THIS IS GOING TO BE GREAT!

I'LL BE THE ONLY ONE AROUND HERE WITH HIS NAME ON A BAT!

THIS WILL REALLY IMPRESS THE KIDS ON THE OTHER TEAMS WE PLAY...THEY'LL BE AFRAID TO SEE ME STEP UP TO THE PLATE ...THEY'LL THINK I'M A BIG-LEAGUER, AND I'LL...

HERE'S YOUR BAT, CHARLIE BROWN!

I HAD A LITTLE TROUBLE WITH THE WOOD-BURNING SET...

HOW SHALL WE PITCH THIS NEXT GUY, CHARLIE BROWN?

WELL, I DON'T KNOW..

THROW HIM YOUR CURVE, CHARLIE BROWN

SAY, HAVE YOU NOTICED HOW BUILT-UP IT'S GETTING AROUND HERE? PRETTY SOON THERE WON'T BE ANY PLACE FOR US TO PLAY..LOOK AT ALL THE HOUSES...

MY GRAMPA SAYS THAT ALL OF THIS USED TO BE A BIG PASTURE..

HE SAYS HE CAN REMEMBER WHEN THEY USED TO DRIVE CATTLE RIGHT ACROSS HERE

MY DAD SAYS HE COULD HAVE MADE A LOT OF MONEY IF HE HAD BOUGHT THIS LAND TWENTY YEARS AGO

TWENTY YEARS AGO? FIVE YEARS AGO WOULD HAVE BEEN ENOUGH!

THAT'S WHAT I SAY!

OF COURSE! LAND VALUES ARE GOING UP EVERYWHERE

LOOK AT THAT PLACE WHERE THEY PUT UP THE NEW SUPER-MARKET..

THAT'S WHAT MY GRAMPA WAS TALKING ABOUT..HE SAID YOU COULD HAVE BOUGHT THAT PROPERTY FOR ALMOST NOTHING ONLY TWO YEARS AGO!

WHAT DO YOU THINK, CHARLIE BROWN?

FRANKLY, I THINK HE'D HIT A CURVE BALL...

BONK!

I CAN'T STAND IT!

 OKAY, LUCY, WHERE WERE YOU ON THAT FLY BALL? LET'S START PAYING ATTENTION!

BLEAH!

 AND HOW ABOUT YOU? YOU WERE OUT OF POSITION ON THAT DOUBLE-PLAY BALL! YOU BETTER LOOK ALIVE!

 BLEAH!

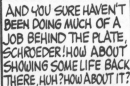 AND YOU SURE HAVEN'T BEEN DOING MUCH OF A JOB BEHIND THE PLATE, SCHROEDER! HOW ABOUT SHOWING SOME LIFE BACK THERE, HUH? HOW ABOUT IT?

 BLEAH!

 MAYBE I WAS TOO HARD ON THEM...AFTER ALL, I HAVEN'T BEEN DOING TOO WELL MYSELF...IN FACT, MY PITCHING HAS BEEN LOUSY!

 BY GOLLY, CHARLIE BROWN, YOU'D BETTER START PITCHING BETTER BALL!! YOU'D BETTER BUCKLE DOWN OUT HERE!

 BLEAH!

SCHULZ

RIGHT IN THE MIDDLE OF A BALL GAME?

ARE YOU OUT OF YOUR MIND?!

I'M TRYING TO PITCH, CAN'T YOU SEE THAT?!! I'VE GOT TO CONCENTRATE ON WHAT I'M DOING!

OH, NOW YOU'RE GOING TO BE HURT, AREN'T YOU? OH, GOOD GRIEF, ALL RIGHT... COME HERE...

SKRITCH SKRITCH SKRITCH SKRITCH SKRITCH

SIGH!

NO WONDER SANDY KOUFAX RETIRED!

LET'S HUSTLE A LITTLE MORE ON THOSE FLY-BALLS!

C'MON! MOVE IN ON THOSE GROUNDERS! THROW THE BALL! DON'T HANG ON TO IT!

ALL RIGHT! EVERYBODY OVER HERE ON THE DOUBLE! LET'S GO!

OKAY, TEAM, THIS IS THE START OF A NEW SEASON, AND I HAVE A FEW WORDS TO SAY..

NOW, I THINK NO ONE WILL DENY THAT SPIRIT PLAYS AN IMPORTANT ROLE IN WINNING BALL GAMES..

SOME MIGHT SAY THAT IT PLAYS THE MOST IMPORTANT ROLE..

THE DESIRE TO WIN IS WHAT MAKES A TEAM GREAT.. WINNING IS EVERYTHING!

THE ONLY THING THAT MATTERS IS TO COME IN FIRST PLACE!

WHAT I'M TRYING TO SAY IS THAT NO ONE EVER REMEMBERS WHO COMES IN SECOND PLACE!

I DO, CHARLIE BROWN... IN 1928, THE GIANTS AND PHILADELPHIA FINISHED SECOND.. IN 1929, IT WAS PITTSBURGH AND THE YANKEES.. IN 1930, IT WAS CHICAGO AND WASHINGTON.. IN 1931, IT WAS THE GIANTS AND THE YANKEES.. IN 1932, IT WAS PITTSBURGH AND...

AND ANOTHER GREAT SEASON GETS UNDERWAY!

  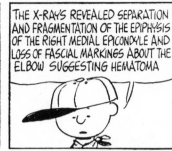 

DEAR PENCIL-PAL, THIS IS THE FIRST DAY I HAVE HAD MY ARM OUT OF A SLING.

I HAVE BEEN SUFFERING FROM "LITTLE LEAGUER'S ELBOW."

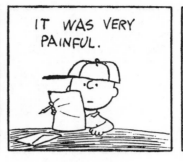

IT WAS VERY PAINFUL.

FOR ME, THAT IS. NOT MY TEAM !!!

YOUR NOSE IS STILL WARM, SNOOPY...

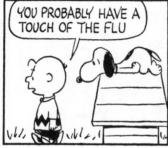

YOU PROBABLY HAVE A TOUCH OF THE FLU

THAT'S A RELIEF...

I WAS AFRAID I MIGHT HAVE "LITTLE LEAGUE ELBOW"!

WHAT HAPPENED TO YOUR ARM? IT'S OUT OF THE SLING!

OH, YES, WHEN A PERSON HAS "LITTLE LEAGUER'S ELBOW," HIS ARM IS IN A SLING FOR ONLY A SHORT PERIOD OF TIME...

DON'T TELL ME YOU'RE READY TO PITCH AGAIN?! OH, NO... NOT FOR AWHILE YET...

WOW! YOU REALLY HAD ME WORRIED THERE FOR A MINUTE!

I FEEL GUILTY, CHARLIE BROWN...

I DON'T WANT TO BE A PITCHING HERO AT YOUR EXPENSE... IF YOU HADN'T GOT "LITTLE LEAGUER'S ELBOW," I WOULDN'T EVEN BE PITCHING

THAT'S ALL RIGHT... THE ONLY THING THAT MATTERS IS THE TEAM... THE TEAM IS EVERYTHING!

OF COURSE, IF YOU WANT TO FEEL JUST A **LITTLE** BIT GUILTY, GO RIGHT AHEAD

HOW'S YOUR ARM, CHARLIE BROWN?

OH, IT FEELS BETTER, THANK YOU... I THINK IT'S GETTING BETTER EVERY DAY...

DO YOU REALIZE WE HAVEN'T LOST A GAME SINCE YOU HAD TO STOP PITCHING? YES, I REALIZE THAT...

HOW'S YOUR ARM, CHARLIE BROWN?

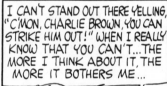

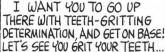

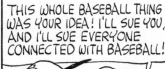

TODAY, TEAM WE FACE THE BEGINNING OF A NEW SEASON..

THE SUCCESS OF A TEAM DEPENDS A LOT UPON ITS ATTITUDE...

DO YOU ALL FEEL THAT WE CAN LOOK FORWARD TO THIS SEASON WITH REAL ANTICIPATION?

NO, WE'RE LOOKING **FORWARD** TO IT WITH REAL HORROR!

THERE IS MUCH TO BE LEARNED FROM BASEBALL BEYOND MERE PLAY..

THE GAME OF BASEBALL AND THE GAME OF LIFE ARE VERY SIMILAR

THE WAY A PERSON PERFORMS UPON THE FIELD MAY BE THE SAME WAY HE PERFORMS IN THE GAME OF LIFE

DON'T SAY THAT!

TODAY I WANT TO TALK TO YOU ABOUT SOMETHING VERY IMPORTANT..

AS YOU KNOW, THE PURPOSES OF SPRING TRAINING ARE MANY AND VARIED...

ONE OF THE MAIN PURPOSES IS TO GET RID OF SOME OF THAT WINTER FAT..

I DIDN'T COME HERE TO BE INSULTED!

HEY, MANAGER, WE HAVE AN IDEA TO IMPROVE THE OUTFIELD

IT'S TOO BARE OUT THERE..ALL YOU SEE IS GRASS...WHAT WE NEED IS SOME FLOWERS AND SHRUBBERY TO MAKE IT LOOK NICE

WE THOUGHT YOU'D WANT TO KNOW SO YOU COULD DO SOMETHING ABOUT IT...

I'M THE ONLY MANAGER WHO GETS A REPORT FROM A GARDEN COMMITTEE!

I JUST WANT TO TELL YOU ALL HOW PLEASED I AM WITH THE SPIRIT YOU'VE BEEN SHOWING..

I LIKE THE WAY YOU'RE TALKING IT UP OUT THERE.. I LIKE TO HEAR LOTS OF CHATTER

DON'T BE SO POLITE, CHARLIE BROWN...

WHY DON'T YOU JUST COME RIGHT OUT AND SAY YOU'RE GLAD YOU HAVE A TEAM OF LOUDMOUTHS?!

THAT'S THE FIFTH FLY BALL YOU'VE DROPPED THIS INNING! WHAT'S THE MATTER WITH YOU?!

I'M SORRY, CHARLIE BROWN...I'M NOT MYSELF THESE DAYS...MY MOTHER TOOK AWAY OUR TV SET AT HOME, AND I'VE BEEN KIND OF UPSET...

MY HANDS SHAKE ALL THE TIME, AND MY THROAT HURTS...

I THINK I'M GOING THROUGH WITHDRAWAL!

THIS IS OUR FIRST GAME OF THE SEASON, CHARLIE BROWN...

YOU'RE OUR MANAGER... TELL US WE'RE NOT GOING TO LOSE!

TELL US, MANAGER, PLEASE TELL US WE'RE NOT GOING TO LOSE! TELL US! TELL US! TELL US WE'RE NOT GOING TO LOSE!

ALL RIGHT...WE'RE NOT GOING TO LOSE!

HA!

ALL RIGHT, HERE WE GO... THE FIRST PITCH OF THE SEASON!

I HAVE TO GET THIS FIRST ONE RIGHT OVER THE PLATE... RIGHT OVER THE OL' PLATE...

THERE IT IS...RIGHT OVER THE PLATE...

...AND CLEAR OVER THE BACKSTOP!

WHAT KIND OF A PITCHER ARE YOU?

YOU THREW THE FIRST BALL OF THE SEASON CLEAR OVER THE BACKSTOP!

IT SORT OF GOT AWAY FROM ME..

WELL, TRY TO BE MORE CAREFUL...

YOU ALMOST HIT MY MOTHER!

I GOT IT! NO, I GOT IT! NO, I GOT IT! I GOT IT!

WHO'S GOT IT? I GOT IT! YOU GOT IT! HE'S GOT IT! THEY GOT IT! YOU GOT IT! I GOT IT! WE GOT IT! I GOT IT!

PLOP!

IT ALWAYS TAKES A FEW GAMES BEFORE MY FIELDERS GET REALLY ORGANIZED!

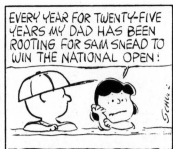

 CHARLIE BROWN, I JUST WANT TO TELL YOU NOT TO FEEL BAD ABOUT WHAT HAPPENED

 WE ALL KNOW HOW TERRIBLE YOU MUST FEEL ABOUT BALKING, AND LETTING IN THE WINNING RUN..

 EVERYONE KNOWS YOU FEEL BAD ABOUT DOING SUCH A STUPID THING AND MAKING SUCH A BONEHEAD PLAY, AND LOSING THE CHAMPIONSHIP...

 AND WE KNOW THAT YOU KNOW IT WAS THE MOST DIM-WITTED CEMENT-HEADED THING A PITCHER COULD DO NO MATTER HOW MANY STUPID BLOCKHEADED THINGS HE MAY HAVE DONE IN.. good grief!

 GET OUT! GET WAY OUT!!

 LET'S TRY TO GET IN ON THOSE!

 WELL, WE LOST AGAIN, BUT IT WASN'T YOUR FAULT, SNOOPY..

 HERE'S YOUR BONE..

 ALL I NEED IS ONE MORE GOOD SEASON, AND I CAN CASH THEM IN AND BUY A BOWLING ALLEY!

 RATS! ANOTHER GAME LOST!

 I REALLY THOUGHT WE WERE GOING TO WIN THIS ONE...

 FOR ONE BRIEF MOMENT VICTORY WAS WITHIN OUR GRASP!

 AND THEN THE GAME STARTED!

 I QUIT! I REFUSE TO PLAY ANY MORE ON A TEAM THAT NEVER WINS!

 DON'T QUIT, VIOLET! PLEASE! WE NEED YOU! WE NEED TO STICK TOGETHER AS A TEAM!

 AFTER ALL, IT'S NOT THE WINNING THAT COUNTS...THE FUN IS IN THE PLAYING!

 OH, BROTHER!

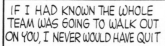

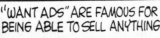

GOOD GRIEF! ANOTHER HOME RUN!

BOY, I MUST BE STUPID TO STAND OUT HERE, AND TAKE A BEATING LIKE THIS!

MY TEAM HATES ME, I'M A LOUSY PITCHER, MY STOMACH HURTS..... I DON'T KNOW WHY I PLAY THIS GAME..I MUST REALLY BE STUPID!

CHARLIE BROWN, YOU CAN'T GO ON LIKE THIS..YOU'VE GOT TO CHANGE YOUR ATTITUDE! THE YEARS ARE GOING BY, AND YOU'RE NOT ENJOYING LIFE AT ALL!

JUST REMEMBER, CHARLIE BROWN...THE MOMENTS YOU SPEND OUT HERE ON THIS PITCHER'S MOUND ARE MOMENTS TO BE TREASURED!

WE'RE NOT GOING TO BE KIDS FOREVER, CHARLIE BROWN SO TREASURE THESE MOMENTS...

POW!

THIS IS A DIFFICULT MOMENT TO TREASURE!

SCHULZ

THIS GUY SAYS FOR ME TO TELL YOU THAT IF YOU THROW ANYTHING THAT EVEN **LOOKS** LIKE IT MIGHT BE A BEAN-BALL, HE'S GOING TO COME OUT HERE AND POUND YOU RIGHT INTO THE GROUND!

I THINK THEY'RE BEGINNING TO GET TO ME...I NEED A NEW PITCH OR SOMETHING...WHAT DO YOU THINK I NEED, SCHROEDER?

A CONCRETE PILL BOX!

OW!

WHAT HAPPENED? WHAT'S THE MATTER?

I GOT HIT ON THE FINGER WITH A FOUL TIP...

IS IT GOING TO BE ALL RIGHT? ARE YOU GOING TO BE ABLE TO PLAY?

I'M NOT SURE..... I'LL HAVE TO FIND OUT.

IT'S ALL RIGHT...I CAN PLAY!

THAT ISN'T EXACTLY WHAT I MEANT

IT'S STARTING TO RAIN, CHARLIE BROWN... AREN'T WE GOING TO CALL THE GAME?

NO, WE'RE NOT GOING TO CALL THE GAME, SO YOU MIGHT AS WELL GET BACK OUT THERE IN CENTER FIELD WHERE YOU BELONG!

AND TRY TO PAY ATTENTION TO WHAT YOU'RE DOING!

POW!

BONK

THIS IS GOING TO BE ANOTHER GREAT SEASON!

CARMANGAY PUBLIC LIBRARY

This book may be kept until the last date stamped below.

A fine will be imposed if kept beyond that time.

DUE	DUE	DUE	DUE
Oc 8 '87			
Fe 17 '88			
Se 6 '88			
Oc 11 '89			
Ja 30 '90			
Ap 1 '90			
No 7 '90			
Fe 14 91			
Jn 9 91			
No 4 92			
Se 1 93			